Footprints 3

Activity Book

My name is _____

	Introduction	page 2
	1 My day	page 4
	2 People and food	page 14
	3 My community	page 24
	4 People and possessions	page 34
	5 A world of sport	page 44
	6 Feelings and health	page 54
	7 Yesterday	page 64
	8 Things in the past	page 74
	9 Things I like doing	page 84
	Cut-outs	page 95

Carol Read

Introduction

Lesson 1

1 🎧 **Listen and circle.**

1	Name:	Sue	(Kim)
2	Age:	eight	nine
3	Address:	13, Lime Street	30, Lime Street
4	Phone number:	407 6329	407 6325
5	Favourite colour:	green	purple
6	Favourite animal:	cat	guinea pig

2 Read and write.

> What's your address?   How old are you?   What's your favourite colour?
> Where do you live?   What's your name?

1 <u>What's your name?</u>   I'm Jack.
2 _____?   I'm eight years old.
3 _____?   I live in Wakeford.
4 _____?   It's 42, Dean Street.
5 _____?   It's red.

3 Read, write and say.

I'm Emily. I'm nine years old.
I live in Wakeford. My address is
42, Dean Street. My phone number is
0825 231 4062. My favourite colour
is blue. My favourite animal is a pony.

I'm _____. I'm _____
years old. I live in _____.
My address is _____.
My phone number is _____.
My favourite colour is _____.
My favourite animal is a _____.

Lesson 1 Introduction

Lesson 2

4 Read and write the story summary.

> emerald   ~~treasure~~   plan   lights   ship   exhibition

The magic emerald

There's an exhibition of (1) ___treasure___ from an old pirate (2) _____. Sam, Jack and Emily go to the (3) _____. They look at the magic (4) _____. But Davina Danger and Freddie Fish have got a (5) _____. The lights go out. The (6) _____ go on again. The magic emerald isn't there.

5 Look and write.

1 What's her name?   She's _____.
2 What's her address?   It's _____.
3 What's her phone number? It's _____.

4 What's his name?   _____.
5 What's his address?   _____.
6 What's his phone number? _____.

6 Listen, find out and write.

Davina

Her favourite colour is _____.
_____ favourite animal _____.

Freddie

His favourite colour is _____.
_____ favourite animal _____.

1 My day

Lesson 1

1 Look and write.

> go to bed ~~go to school~~ do your homework get up
> have lunch get dressed have break go home

1. go to school
2. _____
3. _____
4. _____
5. _____
6. _____
7. _____
8. _____

2 Read and write *Yes, I do* or *No, I don't*.

1. Do you have breakfast in the morning? _____
2. Do you go to bed in the morning? _____
3. Do you get up in the afternoon? _____
4. Do you go home in the afternoon? _____
5. Do you go to school in the evening? _____
6. Do you do your homework in the evening? _____

3 Write sentences about you.

Morning

I wake up.
_____
_____
_____

Evening

_____
_____
_____
_____

Lesson 1 Vocabulary presentation

Lesson 2

4 Read and circle.

1 Davina has got a cat. **True** False
2 Freddie is at Davina's house. True False
3 Freddie phones Davina. True False
4 Freddie and Davina arrange to meet for dinner. True False
5 Davina hears a noise in the garden. True False
6 Sam, Jack and Emily get very wet. True False

5 Read and write the story summary.

millionaires   lunch   ~~breakfast~~   garden   wet   house

At Davina's house

Sam, Jack and Emily have (1) _breakfast_ and go to Davina's (2) _____. Davina and Freddie have got the magic emerald. They're (3) _____. Freddie phones Davina and they arrange to meet for (4) _____. Suddenly Davina hears Rusty in the (5) _____. Sam, Jack, Emily and Rusty hide. Davina looks for them but she gets very (6) _____. It's a lucky escape!

6 Circle, write and say.

eleven o'clock

twelve o'clock

one o'clock

two o'clock

Freddie: What time do you have lunch?

Davina: I always have lunch at _____.

Freddie: Fine. Let's meet at _____ then. Bye.

Lesson 3

7 Look and write the times.

1 ____seven o'clock____ 2 ____half past nine____ 3 _____

4 _____ 5 _____ 6 _____

8 Look, write and say the grammar rap.

What time do you _get up?_ _____

At _____ .

I always _____ .

What time _____ ?

At _____ .

But I sometimes _____ .

When _____ ?

At _____ .

And I never _____ .

9 Write questions and answers.

1 (get up) _What time do you get up?_ _____ At _____ .

2 (have breakfast) When _____ ? At _____ .

3 (have break) _____ ? _____ .

4 (have lunch) _____ ? _____ .

5 (go home) _____ ? _____ .

6 (go to bed) _____ ? _____ .

Lesson 3 Communication and grammar

Lesson 4

10 **Listen, colour and write.**

red = never   orange = sometimes   green = always

1
I <u>always get up at 7 o'clock.</u>

2
I _____.

3
I _____.

4
_____.

5
_____.

6
_____.

11 Write true and false sentences about you.

True

<u>I always go to school at half past eight.</u>
_____.
_____.

False

<u>I sometimes go to bed at one o'clock.</u>
_____.
_____.

12 Order, write and say.   **Pronunciation gem**

sometimes / sister / school /I/ on / cycle / my / Saturday / with / to

I _____.

Lesson 4 Communication grammar and pronunciation

Lesson 5

13 Read and match.

1 Everybody …
2 Sleep gives you energy …
3 Sleep helps you remember …
4 Sleep helps you stay …
5 When you have enough sleep, …
6 When you don't have enough sleep, …

a you feel tired.
b healthy.
c you feel in a good mood.
d for the next day.
e needs sleep.
f what you learn.

14 Look and write.

ten   eight   nine   ~~fifteen~~   seven

1 Babies need about ____fifteen____ hours of sleep a day.
2 Children need about _____ hours of sleep a day.
3 Teenagers need about _____ hours of sleep a day.
4 Adults need about _____ hours of sleep a day.
5 Old people need about _____ hours of sleep a day.

15 Ask, write and say.

Name	When do you go to bed?	What time do you wake up?	How many hours do you sleep?
Me			

Lesson 6

16 Read and write *Always* or *Never*.

1 ____Always____ do an activity to relax before you go to bed.
2 _____ drink cola or other fizzy drinks.
3 _____ eat a big dinner.
4 _____ keep your bedroom quiet and dark.
5 _____ play computer games.
6 _____ go to bed at the same time every day.

17 🎧 Listen, match and write.

What do Jack and Emily do to help them go to sleep?

1 I ____always____ read a book in bed.
2 I _____ have a glass of milk.
3 I _____ listen to quiet music.
4 I _____ have a warm shower.
5 I _____ watch TV.
6 I _____ play computer games.
7 I _____ eat a banana.
8 I _____ listen to a story.

18 Write sentences about you. Use *always*, *sometimes* or *never*.

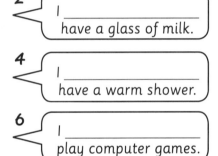
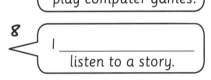

1 _I always drink a glass of milk._
2 _____.
3 _____.
4 _____.
5 _____.
6 _____.

Lesson 6 Content and personalisation

Lesson 7

19 Read, write and act out. Look at Pupil's Book page 12.

Leo

1 What time do you wake up, Leo?
   <u>At seven o'clock.</u>

2 When do you have breakfast?
   _____.

3 When do you go to school?
   _____.

4 What time do you go home?
   _____.

5 What time do you have dinner?
   _____.

6 What time do you go to bed?
   _____.

20 Read and write.

> bed   ~~breakfast~~   school   computer club   morning break
> dinner   afternoon break   lunch   home

I get up at 7.30 and have (1) __breakfast__ at 8 o'clock.
I go to (2) _____ at 8.30. At school I have
(3) _____ at 11 o'clock, (4) _____
at 1 o'clock and (5) _____ at 3 o'clock.
After school I always go to (6) _____.
I go (7) _____ at 4.30. I have (8) _____
at 6.30 and I go to (9) _____ at 8 o'clock. By Amy.

21 Write about your day. Draw a picture.

<u>I get up at</u> _____.
_____.
_____.
_____.
_____.

Lesson 7 Intercultural learning

Lesson 8

22 Look and write the dialogue.

23 Put on the *Grammar Footprints* stickers.

24 Write the answers to the Footprints quiz.

1 Name six daily routines.

 get up   _____    _____

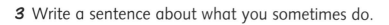

2 Write a sentence about what you always do.

_____.

3 Write a sentence about what you sometimes do.

_____.

4 Write a sentence about what you never do.

_____.

5 What time do you get up?

_____.

6 When do you go to bed?

_____.

7 Write a question to ask someone when they have breakfast.

_____?

8 Write a question to ask someone when they go to school.

_____?

Assess your work.

My Unit 1 score is: _____ / 10

My work is: _____

I need to: _____

Date: _____

Unit 1

Well done!

Woof!

1 My bilingual dictionary

Main vocabulary

wake up _____

get up _____

get dressed _____

have breakfast _____

go to school _____

have break _____

have lunch _____

go home _____

do your homework _____

have dinner _____

get undressed _____

go to bed _____

Other words

morning _____

evening _____

millionaire _____

lucky _____

escape _____

believe _____

Extra words I want to remember

In English	In my language
_____	_____
_____	_____
_____	_____
_____	_____
_____	_____
_____	_____
_____	_____
_____	_____
_____	_____
_____	_____
_____	_____
_____	_____

Footprints fact file: My key words

rest _____

energy _____

good mood _____

bad mood _____

pay attention _____

concentrate _____

healthy _____

relax _____

2 People and food

Lesson 1

1 Look and write.

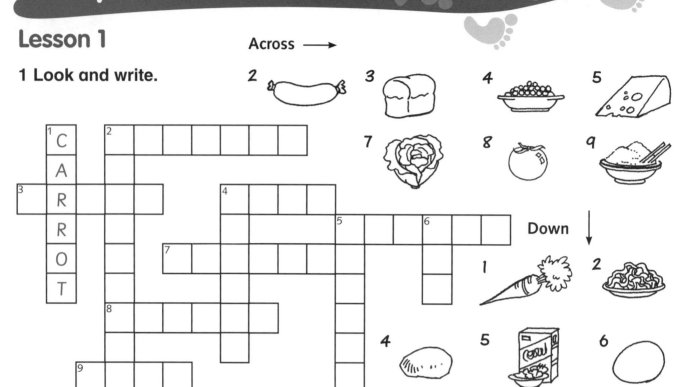

2 Write answers and draw your favourite food.

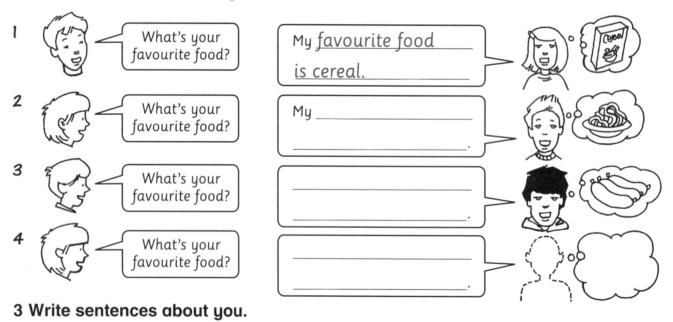

1. My <u>favourite food is cereal.</u>
2. My _____.
3. _____.
4. _____.

3 Write sentences about you.

I like ...   I don't like ...

_____.   _____.

_____.   _____.

_____.   _____.

Lesson 1 Vocabulary presentation

Lesson 2

4 Read and number in order.

a The waiter drops the ice cream. ☐
b Davina walks into town. [1]
c Davina orders lunch. ☐
d Davina walks out of the restaurant. ☐
e The magic emerald falls on the floor. ☐
f Davina goes into a restaurant. ☐

5 Read and write the story summary.

> restaurant   lunch   park   emerald   ~~town~~   ice cream   angry

The enormous ice cream

It's half past eleven. Davina walks into (1) ___town___ and goes into a (2) _____. She orders (3) _____. The waiter trips and drops the (4) _____. The magic (5) _____ falls on the floor. Davina is very (6) _____ and walks out of the restaurant. Sam, Jack and Emily follow Davina to the (7) _____.

6 Read, write and say.

Emily: Oh, look! I think Davina likes ___sausages___.

Jack: Yes, but she doesn't like _____.

Sam: Does Davina like _____?

Emily: No, she doesn't.

Sam: Does she like _____?

Jack: Yes, she does. And I think Davina's favourite food is _____!

Lesson 3

7 Write about your friends.

Natalia likes cheese.
_____.
_____.

Ahmed doesn't like milk.
_____.
_____.

8 Look, write and say the grammar rap.

Sam likes __carrots__ but _____ doesn't like _____.
Does _____? Yes, _____.
_____? No, _____.
_____!

9 Write questions and answers.

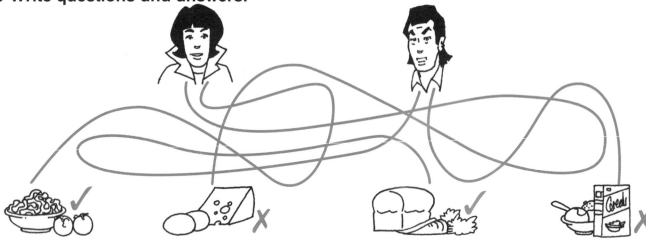

1 (Davina/spaghetti) __Does Davina like spaghetti?__   __Yes, she does.__
2 (Davina/eggs) _____? _____.
3 (Davina/tomatoes) _____? _____.
4 (Freddie/carrots) _____? _____.
5 (Freddie/cereal) _____? _____.
6 (Freddie/ice cream) _____? _____.

Lesson 3 Communication and grammar

Lesson 4

10 Write questions and answers. Look at Pupil's Book page 17.

1 (Sam/guitar) <u>Does Sam play the guitar?</u>   <u>Yes, he does.</u>
2 (Emily/guitar) <u>Does Emily play the guitar?</u>   <u>No, she doesn't.</u>
3 (Jack/piano) _____ ?   _____ .
4 (Sam/drums) _____ ?   _____ .
5 (Emily/tennis) _____ ?   _____ .
6 (Jack/basketball) _____ ?   _____ .

11 Write sentences.

| Emily | piano ✗ | guitar ✓ | Sam | guitar ✓ | drums ✗ |
| Jack | piano ✓ | basketball ✗ | Emily | tennis ✗ | football ✓ |

1 Emily <u>plays the guitar but she doesn't play the piano.</u>
2 Sam _____ .
3 Jack _____ .
4 Emily _____ .

12 Look, write and say.   *Pronunciation gem*

chips, biscuit, crisps, peas, meat, ~~cheese~~, milk, pizza, sandwich, chicken, ice cream, fish

cheese _____

Lesson 4 Communication, grammar and pronunciation   17

Lesson 5

13 Read and circle.

1	You need to eat very little fat	(True)	False
2	You need to eat a lot of sugar.	True	False
3	You need to eat fruit every day.	True	False
4	You need to eat sweets every day.	True	False
5	You need to eat a lot of cereals.	True	False
6	You need to eat very little fish.	True	False

14 Look and write.

~~fats, oils and sugar~~   cereals and rice   milk products
meat, fish, eggs, nuts, beans   vegetables   fruit

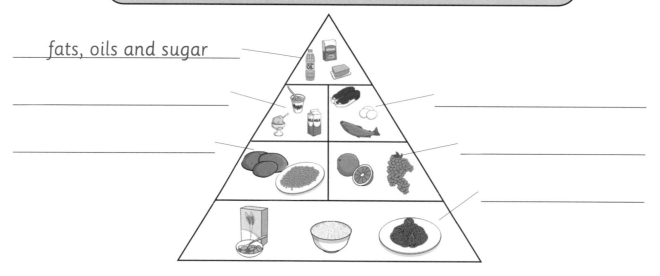

fats, oils and sugar

15 Write sentences about you. Circle your opinion.

1 (for breakfast) _I always eat cereal for breakfast._
2 (for breakfast) _____.
3 (for lunch) _____.
4 (for a snack) _____.
5 (for dinner) _____.

I think my diet is …   very healthy / healthy / not very healthy.

Lesson 5 Content and personalisation

Lesson 6

16 Read and match.

1 You need this to help you grow. — a calcium
2 You need these for your hair, eyes and skin. — b protein
3 You need this for your bones and teeth.   c fibre
4 You need this to keep your body healthy.   d vitamins

17 Write about the food. Look at Pupil's Book page 19.

1 Banana: <u>It's got vitamins and fibre.</u>
2 Milk: _____.
3 Carrot: _____.
4 Bread: _____.
5 Chicken: _____.
6 Cheese: _____.

18 Draw and write.

Choose six foods to take on a healthy picnic!

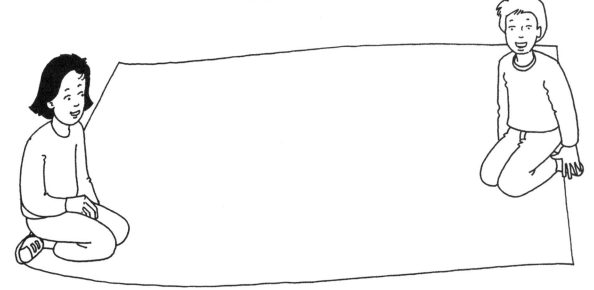

I've got _____, _____, _____, _____, _____ and _____ for my picnic.

Lesson 7

19 Read and complete. Look at Pupil's Book page 20.

	Favourite food	Likes …	Doesn't like …
Leo	baked beans on toast	_____	_____
Oliver	_____	hamburgers and chips, potatoes	_____
Daisy	_____	_____	eggs
Amy	_____	_____	_____

20 Look and write.

1 Leo likes _____ but he doesn't like _____.

2 Oliver _____.

3 Daisy _____.

4 Amy _____.

21 Write and draw.

Shepherd's pie is a favourite food of children in my country. Shepherd's pie has got meat and potatoes. You can eat shepherd's pie on its own or with carrots and peas. It's delicious!

_____
_____
_____
_____
_____

Lesson 7 Intercultural learning

Lesson 8

22 Look and write the dialogue.

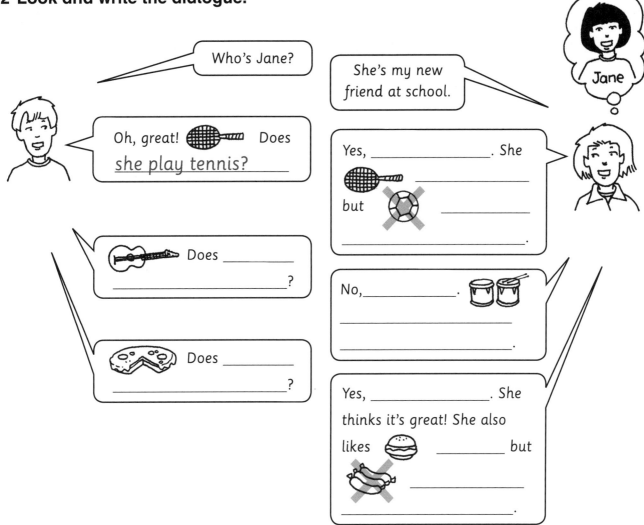

23 Put on the *Grammar Footprints* stickers.

Lesson 8 Unit review

24 Write the answers to the *Footprints quiz*.

1 Name six foods.

    bread   _____   _____

     _____   _____   _____

2 Does Davina like peas?

    _____.

3 Does Freddie like rice?

    _____.

4 Write two questions about Jack and Emily.

    _____?

    _____?

5 Write a sentence about Davina. Use *but*.

    _____.

6 Write a sentence about Sam. Use *but*.

    _____.

7 Name three sections of the food pyramid.

    _____   _____   _____

8 Write a sentence about what you eat to get protein and fibre.

    _____.

Assess your work.

My Unit 2 score is: / 10

My work is: _____

I need to: _____

Unit 2   Date: _____

Well done!

Woof!

Lesson 8 Unit review

2 My bilingual dictionary

Main vocabulary

bread _____

cereal _____

cheese _____

egg _____

spaghetti _____

rice _____

sausage _____

peas _____

potato _____

carrot _____

lettuce _____

tomato _____

Other words

waiter _____

restaurant _____

bark _____

wait _____

order _____

trip _____

drop _____

angry _____

basketball _____

guitar _____

drums _____

tennis _____

Footprints fact file: My key words

sugar _____

milk products _____

vegetables _____

meat _____

protein _____

vitamin _____

calcium _____

fibre _____

Extra words I want to remember

In English   In my language

_____   _____

_____   _____

_____   _____

_____   _____

_____   _____

_____   _____

_____   _____

3 My community

Lesson 1

1 Look and write.

> supermarket   café   ~~cinema~~   newsagent   post office   bank   hotel   chemist

1 ____cinema____   2 _____   3 _____   4 _____

5 _____   6 _____   7 _____   8 _____

2 Read and write Yes, there is / are or No, there isn't / aren't.

1 Is there a library where you live? _____.

2 Is there a shopping centre? _____.

3 Is there a post office? _____.

4 Are there any shops? _____.

5 Are there any cafés? _____.

6 Are there any hotels? _____.

3 Write sentences about where you live.

1 There's a supermarket but there isn't a post office.

2 There's a _____ but _____.

3 _____.

4 There are shops but there aren't any hotels.

5 There are _____ but _____.

6 _____.

24   Lesson 1 Vocabulary presentation

Lesson 2

4 Read and write the correct sentences.

1 Davina phones Freddie.   No, <u>Freddie phones Davina.</u>
2 Davina is in danger.   No, _____.
3 Freddie has got the magic emerald. No, _____.
4 There's a red car.   No, _____.
5 There's a woman in the car.   No, _____.
6 Z wants to buy the magic emerald. No, _____.

5 Read and write the story summary.

magic   house   bag   supermarket   ~~car park~~   man

The black car

Davina goes to meet Freddie in the (1) <u>car park</u>

opposite the (2) _____.

Davina has got the (3) _____ emerald.

It's safe in her (4) _____.

The name of the (5) _____ in the black car is Q.

Q asks Davina and Freddie to his (6) _____.

6 Read, tick (✓) and say.

Come to my house this evening. Go straight on. Turn left. My house is on the right.

a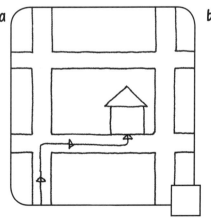

b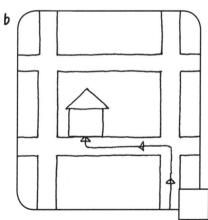

Lesson 2 Language input and story

Lesson 3

7 Look, read and write.

1. Go straight on. Turn left. Turn right. It's on the left.
   It's the ____post office____.
2. Go straight on. Turn right. Turn left. It's on the right.
   It's the _____.
3. Go straight on. Turn right. Turn left. Go past the cinema.
   Turn left. It's opposite the school. It's the _____.

8 Look, write and say the grammar rap.

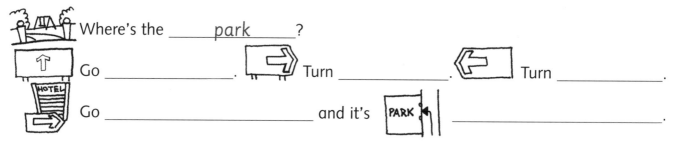

Where's the ____park____?
Go _____. Turn _____. Turn _____.
Go _____ and it's _____.

9 Look and write directions.

1. Where's the supermarket?
   Go ____straight____ on. Turn _____.
   Turn _____. Go _____.
   It's on the _____.
2. Where's the museum?
   Go _____ on. Turn _____.
   Turn _____. Go _____.
   It's on the _____.
3. Where's the newsagent?
   Go _____ on. Turn _____.
   Turn _____. Go _____
   and the _____. Turn _____.
   It's _____ the park.

Lesson 4

10 Look, write and act out.

You: Where's your house, Sam?

Sam: Go ___straight on___. Turn _____.
Turn _____. Go _____.
It's _____.

You: Where's your house, Emily?

Emily: Go _____. Turn _____.
Turn _____. Go _____.
It's _____.

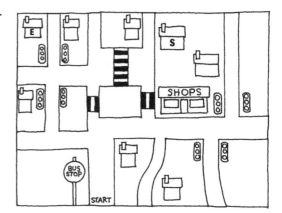

11 Look and write.

Go _____. _____.
_____. _____.
_____.

12 Order, write and say.

Pronunciation gem

in / lovely / lighthouse / the / live / and / the / ~~Luke~~ / left / on / little / Lucy

Luke _____.

Lesson 5

13 Read and match.

1 We all …
2 There are many different …
3 Some forms of transport …
4 Other forms of transport are …
5 It is a good idea to share …
6 It is a good idea to use …

a public transport.
b clean and 'green'.
c car journeys.
d forms of transport.
e use transport.
f cause pollution.

14 Look and write.

bike

motorbike

bus

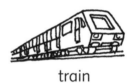
train

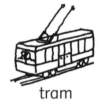
tram

electric car

car

Transport which causes pollution

car
_____
_____
_____

Transport which is clean and 'green'

_____
_____
_____

plane

15 Read and write Yes, I do or No, I don't.

1 Do you go to school by bus?   _____.
2 Do you go to the supermarket by car?   _____.
3 Do you visit friends by train?   _____.
4 Do you go to the cinema by bus?   _____.
5 Do you go to the park by bike?   _____.
6 Do you go on holiday by plane?   _____.

Lesson 6

16 Read and write *car*, *bike*, *bus* **and / or** *train*.

1. Wear bright clothes. _____bike_____
2. Sit in the back. _____
3. Sit down or hold on. _____
4. Wear a helmet. _____
5. Wear a seat belt. _____
6. Use a bell. _____

17 Write about transport you use.

1. When I go to school by _____bus_____, I _____sit down_____.
2. When I go to the supermarket by _____, I _____.
3. When I go to my friend's house by _____, I _____.
4. When I go on holiday by _____, I _____.

18 Draw and write.

Invent a form of transport for the future. Write the safety rules.

Lesson 7

19 Read and write the answers. Look at Pupils Book page 28.

1 Does Leo go to the ice rink on foot? <u>No, he doesn't. He goes by car.</u>

2 Does Amy go to the shopping centre by bike? _____.

3 Does Oliver go to the sports centre by bus? _____.

4 Does Daisy go to the library by car? _____.

20 Match and write sentences.

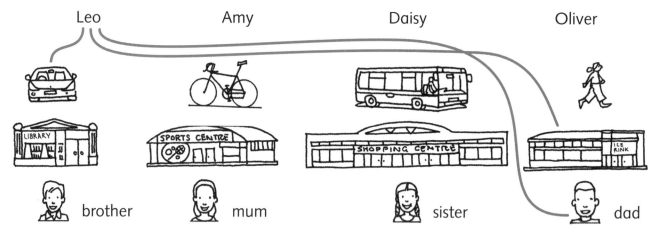

1 Leo <u>goes to the ice rink by car with his dad.</u>

2 Amy _____.

3 Daisy _____.

4 Oliver _____.

21 Write and draw.

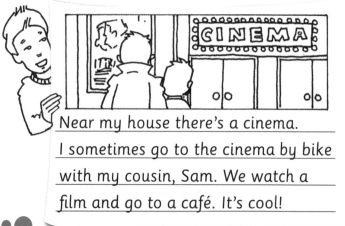

Near my house there's a cinema. I sometimes go to the cinema by bike with my cousin, Sam. We watch a film and go to a café. It's cool!

Lesson 7 Intercultural learning

Lesson 8

22 Look and write the dialogue.

1 Where's the <u>shopping centre</u>?

2 Go _____
Turn _____
Turn _____
Go past the _____
and the _____.
The _____
is on the _____.

3 Do you go to the _____?

4 No, I don't.
I _____.

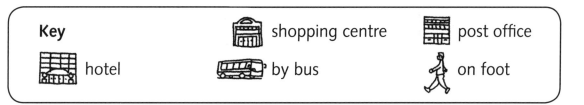

Key — shopping centre — post office — hotel — by bus — on foot

23 Put on the Grammar Footprints stickers.

| | the | cinema? |
| | your | house? |

| | right. |

| Go | | the museum.
| | | the shops. |

| It's | | | the supermarket. |

Lesson 8 Unit review   31

24 Write the answers to the *Footprints quiz*.

1 Name six places in the community.

1. c i n e m a   2. n__ __s__g__ __t   3. c__e__ __s__

4. p__ __ __ o__ __ i__ __   5. b__ __ __   6. h__ __ e__

2 Write two sentences about where you go by car.

_____.

_____.

3 Write two sentences about where you go by bus or train.

_____.

_____.

4 Write a sentence about why we use transport.

_____.

5 Write a sentence about what we can do to look after the environment.

_____.

6 Write two rules you follow when you go by car.

_____.

_____.

7 Write two rules you follow when you go by bike.

_____.

_____.

Assess your work.

My Unit 3 score is: / 10

My work is: _____

I need to: _____

Date: _____

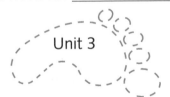

Well done!

Woof!

Lesson 8 Unit review

3 My bilingual dictionary

Main vocabulary

shopping centre _____

cinema _____

supermarket _____

post office _____

library _____

theatre _____

café _____

chemist _____

newsagent _____

museum _____

bank _____

hotel _____

Other words

car park _____

danger _____

safe _____

traffic lights _____

bus stop _____

map _____

lighthouse _____

Extra words I want to remember

In English	In my language
_____	_____
_____	_____
_____	_____
_____	_____
_____	_____
_____	_____
_____	_____
_____	_____
_____	_____
_____	_____
_____	_____
_____	_____

Footprints fact file: My key words

petrol _____

diesel _____

pollution _____

clean _____

journey _____

public transport _____

seat belt _____

helmet _____

4 People and possessions

Lesson 1

1 Look and write.

watch   torch   ~~camera~~   kite   mobile phone   MP3 Player

1 _camera_
2 _____
3 _____
4 _____
5 _____
6 _____

2 Read and write Yes, I have or No, I haven't.

1 Have you got a watch?   _____.
2 Have you got a torch?   _____.
3 Have you got a stamp collection? _____.
4 Have you got a frisbee?   _____.
5 Have you got a kite?   _____.
6 Have you got a camera?   _____.

3 Look and write sentences He's / She's / They've got … .

1 He's got an MP3 player.
2 _____.
3 _____.
4 _____.
5 _____.
6 _____.

Lesson 1 Vocabulary presentation

Lesson 2

4 Read and circle.

1. Davina and Freddie go to Q's house.   (True)   False
2. Q has got a gem collection.   True   False
3. Q has got a hundred gems.   True   False
4. Rusty takes the magic emerald.   True   False
5. Rusty eats the magic emerald.   True   False
6. Freddie runs away with the magic emerald.   True   False

5 Read and write the story summary.

table   biscuit   collection   gym   emerald   ~~house~~

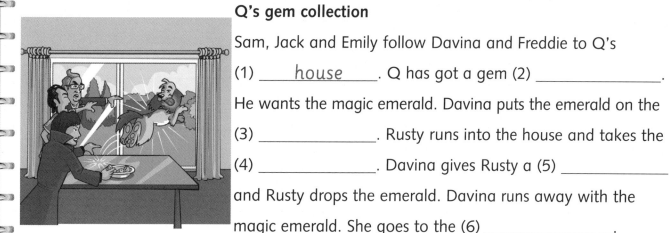

Q's gem collection

Sam, Jack and Emily follow Davina and Freddie to Q's (1) ___house___. Q has got a gem (2) _____. He wants the magic emerald. Davina puts the emerald on the (3) _____. Rusty runs into the house and takes the (4) _____. Davina gives Rusty a (5) _____ and Rusty drops the emerald. Davina runs away with the magic emerald. She goes to the (6) _____.

6 Read and number in order.

Q: Ninety-nine. And with the magic emerald, a hundred. Can I see it now, please? ☐

Freddie: No, it isn't yours, Davina. It's ours. ☐

Davina: Don't worry. I can get the magic emerald. ☐

Q: Whose is the magic emerald? ☐

Davina: It's mine. ☐

Freddie: How many gems have you got? [1]

Lesson 2 Language input and story

Lesson 3

7 Look, read and write.

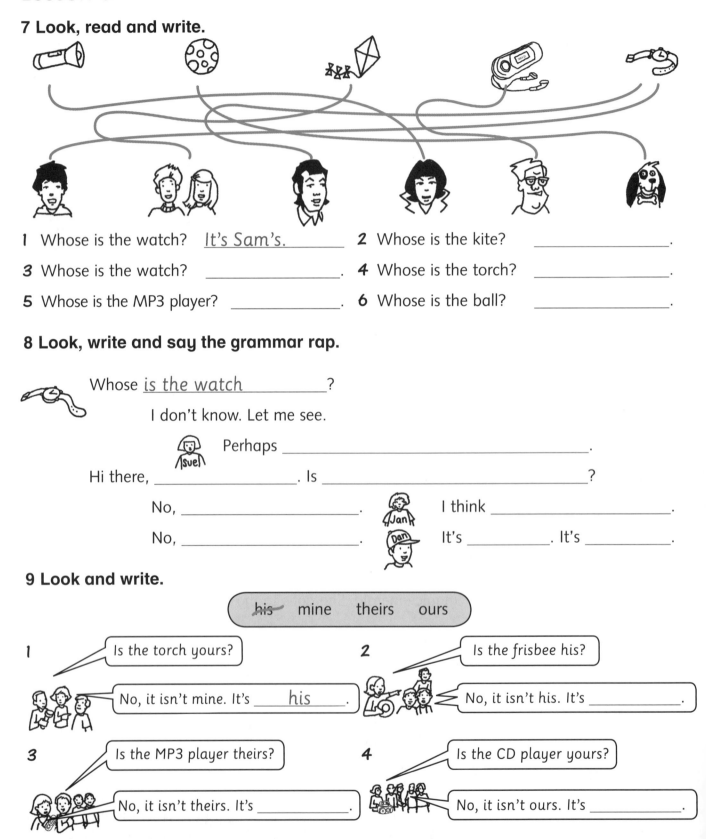

1 Whose is the watch? It's Sam's.   2 Whose is the kite? _____.
3 Whose is the watch? _____. 4 Whose is the torch? _____.
5 Whose is the MP3 player? _____. 6 Whose is the ball? _____.

8 Look, write and say the grammar rap.

Whose is the watch ?
I don't know. Let me see.
Perhaps _____.
Hi there, _____. Is _____?
No, _____.   I think _____.
No, _____.   It's _____. It's _____.

9 Look and write.

his   mine   theirs   ours

1 Is the torch yours?
   No, it isn't mine. It's ___his___.

2 Is the frisbee his?
   No, it isn't his. It's _____.

3 Is the MP3 player theirs?
   No, it isn't theirs. It's _____.

4 Is the CD player yours?
   No, it isn't ours. It's _____.

Lesson 4

10 Match and write the answers.

nineteen   65   thirty-two   32   twenty-one   76
21   ninety-eight   100   fifty-four   forty-three
eighty-seven   seventy-six   87   sixty-five   43
        19   98

What word is missing from the box? _____

What number is missing from the box? _____

11 Write sentences.

 56  32  42  87  61

1 Sam <u>has got fifty-six stamps.</u>

2 Jack _____.

3 Emily _____.

4 Davina _____.

5 Freddie _____.

12 Look, write and say.

 Pronunciation gem

stamps   stickers   torches   watches   kites
key rings   houses   postcards   phones   footprints

/s/   /z/   /ɪz/

kites   _____   _____

_____   _____   _____

_____   _____   _____

                 _____

Lesson 4 Communication, grammar and pronunciation

Lesson 5

13 Read and circle.

1 Many people use computers.   True   False
2 Children don't use computers at school.   True   False
3 People use computers for the same reasons.   True   False
4 At work people use computers to write reports.   True   False
5 At home people use computers to watch DVDs.   True   False
6 People also use computers to connect to the internet.   True   False

14 Look and write.

monitor   mouse   ~~printer~~   keyboard   screen

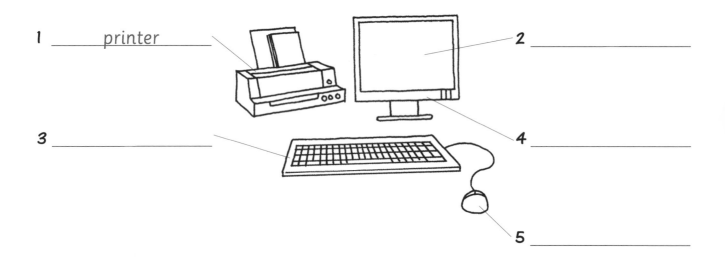

1 ___printer___
2 _____
3 _____
4 _____
5 _____

15 Write sentences about you.

1 <u>I use a computer at home to play games.</u>
2 _____.
3 _____.
4 _____.

Lesson 6

16 Order and write.

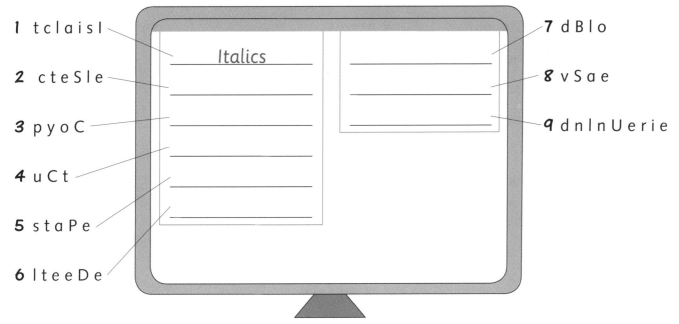

1 t c I a i s l — Italics
2 c t e S l e
3 p y o C
4 u C t
5 s t a P e
6 l t e e D e
7 d B l o
8 v S a e
9 d n I n U e r i e

17 Read and write.

save   close   finish   ~~use~~   open   print   give

When I (1) _____use_____ a computer to do a project at school, I (2) _____ a new document. I (3) _____ my document a title and I (4) _____ my document. When I (5) _____ my project, I save all the changes and (6) _____ or (7) _____ my document.

18 Tick (✔) and write about you.

 stories ☐
 poems ☐
 projects ☐
 letters ☐

I write stories and projects on a computer. I don't write poems or letters on a computer.

Lesson 7

19 Read and write answers. Look at Pupil's Book page 36.

1 Whose is the PlayStation?   It's Amy's.
2 Whose is the CD player?   _____.
3 Whose is the frisbee?   _____.
4 Is the computer Oliver's?   No, it isn't. It's Daisy's.
5 Is the laptop Leo's?   _____.
6 Is the stamp collection Daisy's?   _____.

20 Match and write sentences.

Amy   Oliver   Daisy   Leo

78   49   25   36

1 Amy has got a collection of twenty-five postcards.
2 Oliver _____.
3 Daisy _____.
4 Leo _____.

21 Write and draw.

I've got a sticker collection of wild animals. I've got forty-two stickers. I've also got a kite. I fly my kite in the park with my brother after school. It's great.

Lesson 8

22 Look and write the dialogue.

- Whose is the sticker? Is <u>it Ben's?</u>
- No, _____. It's mine. I've _____ _____.
- Oh, really. How _____ _____?
- Oh, I've got _____ _____. My favourite _____ _____ on it.
- And whose _____ _____?
- Oh, they _____ sister, _____. She's _____ _____.

23 Put on the *Grammar Footprints* stickers.

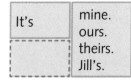

Lesson 8 Unit review 41

24 Write the answers to the *Footprints quiz*.

1 Name the six possessions.

watch _____ _____

_____ _____ _____

2 Write a sentence about Leo's collection.
   _____.

3 Write a sentence about Daisy's collection.
   _____.

4 Write why you use a computer at school.
   _____.

5 Write why people use a computer at home.
   _____.

6 Write two sentences about a collection you've got.
   _____.
   _____.

7 Write two sentences about possessions you've got.
   _____.
   _____.

Assess your work.

My Unit 4 score is: ____ / 10

My work is: _____

I need to: _____

Date: _____

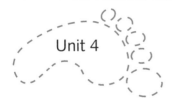
Unit 4

Well done! Woof!

Lesson 8 Unit review

4 My bilingual dictionary

Main vocabulary

watch _____

torch _____

camera _____

frisbee _____

kite _____

mobile phone _____

MP3 player _____

CD player _____

stamps _____

stickers _____

key rings _____

postcards _____

Other words

gem _____

collection _____

fifty-two _____

sixty-three _____

seventy-four _____

(Numbers to 100)

Extra words I want to remember

In English	In my language
_____	_____
_____	_____
_____	_____
_____	_____
_____	_____
_____	_____
_____	_____
_____	_____
_____	_____
_____	_____
_____	_____
_____	_____

Footprints fact file: My key words

keyboard _____

screen _____

printer _____

copy _____

cut _____

paste _____

delete _____

save _____

5 A world of sport

Lesson 1

1 Look and write.

> gymnastics   baseball   golf   judo   windsurfing   rowing   riding   fencing

1 __judo__   2 _____   3 _____   4 _____

5 _____   6 _____   7 _____   8 _____

2 Write and answer *Yes, I can* or *No, I can't*.

1 Can you ski? _____ .

2 _____? _____ .

3 _____? _____ .

4 _____? _____ .

5 _____? _____ .

6 _____? _____ .

3 Look and write sentences. Use *He / She* or *They can ...* .

1   2   3   4   5   6

1 __He can ski.__   2 _____ .

3 _____ . 4 _____ .

5 _____ . 6 _____ .

Lesson 1 Vocabulary presentation

Lesson 2

4 Read, match and say.

What's Davina doing?

1. Davina is running.
2. Davina is riding a bike.
3. Davina is smiling.
4. Davina is drinking water.
5. Davina is looking sleepy.
6. Davina is falling off the bike.

5 Read and write the story summary.

> water   bag   poison   ~~gym~~   bike   mobile phone

Poison!

Sam, Jack and Emily are looking for Davina at the (1) ___gym___.
Freddie also goes to the gym. Freddie walks towards Davina and puts some (2) _____ in her (3) _____.
Davina looks sleepy and falls off the (4) _____.
Freddie takes the magic emerald and Davina's (5) _____ from her (6) _____.

6 Read and number in order.

Sam: Where is he? ☐

Emily: He's putting something into Davina's water! ☐

Jack: Oh, no! Poison! ☐

Jack: Behind the bikes! He's walking towards Davina! ☐

Emily: Hey, I can see Freddie! [1]

Sam: What's he doing now? ☐

Lesson 2 Language input and story

Lesson 3

7 Look, read and write.

1 What's he doing? 2 What's she doing? 3 What are they doing?

He's riding. _____   _____.   _____.

4 What's he doing? 5 What's she doing? 6 What are they doing?

_____.   _____.   _____.

8 Look, write and say the grammar rap.

What 's she doing _____ on channel one?
_____ – it's exciting and fun.

What _____ on channel two?
_____ – it's amazing and cool.

What _____ on channel three?
_____ – it's the channel for me!

9 Look and write.

a    b

1 Ann: She's running. _____   _____.
2 Dan: _____.   _____.
3 Liz: _____.   _____.
4 Ben and Sue: _____.   _____.

Lesson 3 Communication and grammar

Lesson 4

10 Look and match.

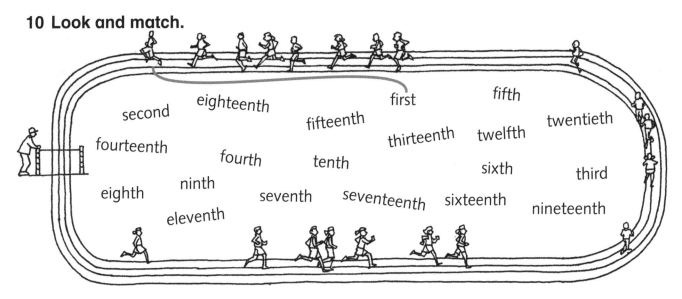

11 Look and write.

I'm first.

12 Look, write and say.

Pronunciation gem

sailing   judo   basketball   volleyball   windsurfing   gymnastics   baseball
riding   karate   tennis

Oo	Ooo	oOo
sailing	_____	_____
_____	_____	_____
_____	_____	
_____		

Lesson 4 Communication, grammar and pronunciation

Lesson 5

13 Read and match.

1 The human body has more than …
2 Our muscles are essential …
3 We have voluntary muscles …
4 Voluntary muscles work when they receive …
5 We have involuntary muscles …
6 Involuntary muscles work …

a in our heart and intestines.
b a message from the brain.
c automatically.
d for everything we do.
e 600 muscles.
f in our arms and legs.

14 Look and write.

neck   hips   arms   back   toes   legs   hands   stomach   face   shoulders

1 _face_
2 _____
3 _____
4 _____
5 _____
6 _____
7 _____
8 _____
9 _____
10 _____

15 Write sentences about you.

1 _I have muscles in my arms._
2 _____ .
3 _____ .
4 _____ .

Lesson 6

16 Look and match.

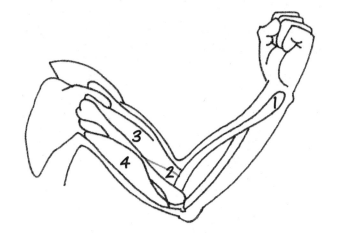

tendon

triceps muscle

biceps muscle

bone

17 Look and write.

~~knees~~   arms   fingers   neck   toes   back

1   2   3   4   5   6

1 Mr Muscle says 'Bend your ____knees____!'   2 Mr Muscle says 'Stretch your _____!'

3 Mr Muscle says 'Bend your _____!'   4 Mr Muscle says 'Move your _____!'

5 My Muscle says 'Bend your _____!'   6 Mr Muscle says 'Move your _____!'

18 Write and draw.

I use my muscles to swim and ride my bike.

_____

_____

Lesson 6 Content and personalisation

Lesson 7

19 Read and write. Look at Pupil's Book page 44.

1 Oliver is at a football match.
2 Amy _____.
3 Leo _____.
4 Daisy _____.

20 Write the questions. Look at Pupil's Book page 44.

1 What's Daisy wearing?   She's wearing a blue swimsuit.
2 _____?   He's wearing a white t-shirt and red shorts.
3 _____?   He's throwing the ball.
4 _____?   She's wearing a black jacket and hat.
5 _____?   He's kicking the ball.
6 _____?   She's riding a grey pony.

21 Draw and write.

This is a picture of me at a junior tennis match. I'm wearing a white t-shirt and blue shorts. I'm hitting the ball. My cousin and my sister are watching the match.

Lesson 7 Intercultural learning

Lesson 8

22 Look and write the dialogue.

What <u>are you doing</u>, Tom?

I'm _____ _____. And I can see Helen.

What's she _____ _____?

_____.

Oh, really? What _____ _____ wearing?

She's _____ _____. And she's sitting next to some friends.

What _____ _____?

They're _____.

23 Put on the *Grammar Footprints* stickers.

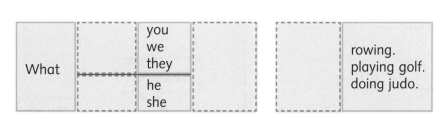

Lesson 8 Unit review

24 Write the answers to the *Footprints quiz*.

1 Name the six sports.

 skiing   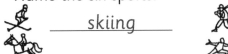 _____    _____

 _____   _____    _____

2 What's Jack doing?

_____.

3 What's Emily doing?

_____.

4 What are they doing on channel 1?

_____.

5 What are they doing on channel 2?

_____.

6 What's Oliver doing? What's he wearing? (Look at Pupil's Book page 44.)

_____.

_____.

7 Write a sentence about where you have muscles.

_____.

8 Write a sentence about what you use your muscles for.

_____.

Assess your work.

My Unit 5 score is: _____ / 10

My work is: _____

I need to: _____

Date: _____

Unit 5

Well done!
Woof!

Lesson 8 Unit review

5 My bilingual dictionary

Main vocabulary

volleyball _____

baseball _____

golf _____

judo _____

karate _____

gymnastics _____

windsurfing _____

skiing _____

sailing _____

rowing _____

riding _____

fencing _____

Other words

poison _____

fit _____

gym _____

sleepy _____

channel _____

race _____

Extra words I want to remember

In English	In my language
_____	_____
_____	_____
_____	_____
_____	_____
_____	_____
_____	_____
_____	_____
_____	_____
_____	_____
_____	_____
_____	_____
_____	_____
_____	_____

Footprints fact file: My key words

muscle _____

(in)voluntary _____

brain _____

tissue _____

tendon _____

bone _____

contract _____

relax _____

6 Feelings and health

Lesson 1

1 Look and write.

2 Write the questions and answers.

1. Are you <u>feeling alright</u>? — No, I'm not. I've got <u>an earache</u>.
2. Are you _____? — No, I'm not. I've got _____.
3. Are you _____? — _____.
4. _____? — _____.

3 Look and write sentences He's / She's got ... .

1. <u>She's got a bruise on her leg.</u>
2. _____
3. _____
4. _____
5. _____
6. _____

Lesson 1 Vocabulary presentation

Lesson 2

4 Read and circle.

1. Davina's got a toothache.   True   (False)
2. Davina's got a headache.   True   False
3. Davina's leg hurts.   True   False
4. Davina's neck hurts.   True   False
5. Davina's feeling hot.   True   False
6. Davina's feeling terrible. True   False

5 Read and write the story summary.

bag   mobile phone   water   number   ~~outside~~   phone call

The gym instructor

Jack and Emily go and see Davina. The gym instructor tells them to wait (1) ___outside___. The gym instructor suggests that Davina drinks some (2) _____ and lies down. Davina asks the gym instructor for her sports (3) _____. The magic emerald and her (4) _____ are missing. Davina sleeps for an hour and asks to make a (5) _____. She can't remember Freddie's phone (6) _____ so she decides to call her phone.

6 Read, write and say.

Thank you   my neck hurts   ~~What's the matter~~   drink this water

Gym instructor: (1) _What's the matter_____?

Davina: I've got a headache, (2) _____ and I'm feeling terrible.

Gym instructor: Why don't you (3) _____ and lie down here.

Davina: (4) _____.

Lesson 2 Language input and story

Lesson 3

7 Look and write.

What's the matter?

1 My <u>neck hurts</u> _____.

2 I've got _____.

3  My _____.

4 _____.

5 _____.

6 _____.

8 Look, write and say the grammar rap.

What's <u>the matter?</u> _____

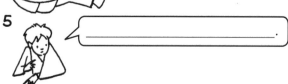 I've _____.

Why don't you _____?

Yes, good idea!

What's _____?

 My _____.

Why _____?

Yes, _____!

9 Look and write.

1  2 3   4 5 6

1 He's <u>got a cold.</u> _____

2 She _____.

3 They _____.

4 _____.

5 _____.

6 _____.

Lesson 4

10 Read, number in order and act out.

Jack: No, I'm not. ☐

Sam: Are you feeling alright, Jack? ☐ 1

Jack: Yes, good idea. ☐

Sam: Oh, poor you. Why don't you lie down and rest for a while? ☐

Sam: What's the matter? ☐

Jack: I've got a tummy ache. ☐

11 Look and write.

take   drink   lie   ~~go~~   put   go

1  Why don't you __go__ to bed?

2 Why don't you _____ your medicine?

3 Why _____ a plaster on it?

4 Why _____ down and rest?

5 _____ some water?

6 _____ to the doctor?

12 Look, write and say.

Pronunciation gem

nose   ~~hot~~   body   shoulder   doctor   toes
broken   phone   stop   watch   bone   box

Cough   Cold

__hot__   _____   _____   _____

_____   _____   _____   _____

_____   _____   _____   _____

Lesson 5

13 Look and write.

~~see~~   taste   hear   touch   smell   nose   ~~eyes~~   ears   tongue   skin

1. We __see__ with our __eyes__.
2. We _____ with our _____.
3. We _____ with our _____.
4. We _____ with our _____.
5. We _____ with our _____.

14 Look and tick (✔).

What senses do you use when you …

	pick a flower?	look at a sunset?	eat a pizza?	stroke a dog?	watch TV?	go for a walk?
sight	✔					
hearing						
touch	✔					
taste						
smell	✔					

15 Write sentences about you.

1. I use my eyes to look at photos.
2. _____
3. _____
4. _____
5. _____
6. _____

Lesson 5 Content and personalisation

Lesson 6

16 Look and match.

1 sweet 2 salty 3 sour 4 bitter

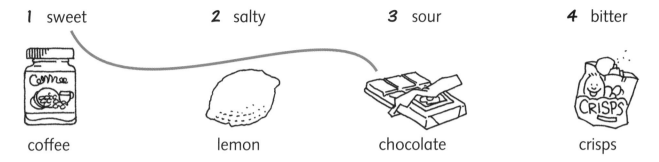

coffee lemon chocolate crisps

17 Read, write and colour.

The sides of the tongue which taste sour things are yellow.
The front of the tongue which tastes sweet and salty things is red.
The back of the tongue which tastes bitter things is green.

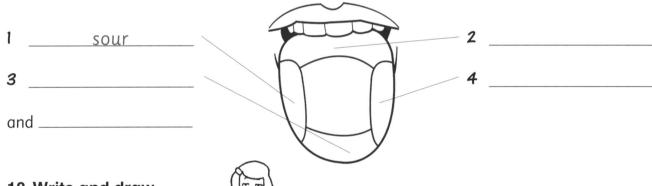

1 ___sour___ 2 _____
3 _____ 4 _____
and _____

18 Write and draw.

I like sweet things such as apples and biscuits. I don't like sour things such as lemons and vinegar.

Lesson 7

19 Read and write the answers. Look at Pupil's page 52.

1 Who goes to the doctor with Daisy?   _Her mum_
2 What does Oliver need to wear?   _____
3 What does the nurse give Amy?   _____
4 Who is very kind?   _____
5 Who looks at Leo's teeth?   _____
6 Who looks at Oliver's eyes?   _____
7 Who tells Amy to lie down and rest?   _____

20 Read and write.

> cough   medicine   home   mum   ~~doctor~~   earache   doctor

I go to the (1) _doctor_ with my (2) _____ when I've got an (3) _____ or a bad (4) _____. The (5) _____ is very kind. She sometimes tells me to take (6) _____ and stay at (7) _____ for a few days. By Daisy.

21 Write about you. Draw a picture.

_____
_____
_____
_____
_____

Lesson 8

22 Look and write the dialogue.

23 Put on the *Grammar Footprints* stickers.

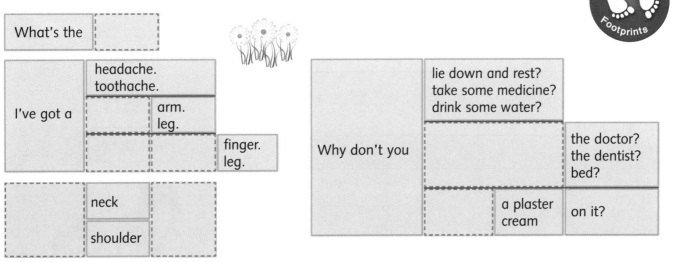

24 Write the answers to the *Footprints quiz*.

1 Name the six ailments.

toothache _____ _____ _____

_____ _____ _____

2 Ask and write what's the matter.

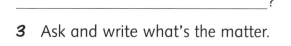

_____? _____.

3 Ask and write what's the matter.

_____? _____.

4 Ask and write what's the matter.

_____? _____.

5 Sam's got flu. Suggest what to do.

_____

6 Davina's got a headache. Suggest what to do.

_____

7 Write about your five senses.

 _____ _____

_____. _____.

8 Write a sentence about what you use your senses to do.

_____

Assess your work.

My Unit 6 score is: ___ / 10

My work is: _____

I need to: _____

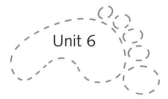
Unit 6

Date: _____

Well done! Woof!

Lesson 8 Unit review

6 My bilingual dictionary

Main vocabulary

headache _____

tummy ache _____

earache _____

backache _____

toothache _____

bruise _____

cut _____

cough _____

cold _____

flu _____

temperature _____

broken arm _____

Other words

alright _____

terrible _____

go away _____

instructor _____

wait _____

lie down _____

better _____

plaster _____

cream _____

doctor _____

Footprints fact file: My key words

hear _____

smell _____

touch _____

taste _____

tongue _____

salty _____

bitter _____

sour _____

Extra words I want to remember

In English	In my language
_____	_____
_____	_____
_____	_____
_____	_____
_____	_____
_____	_____
_____	_____
_____	_____

7 Yesterday

Lesson 1

1 Look and write.

w n t o
1 _____town_____

i c r s u c
2 _____

e h c a b
3 _____

u r f n a i f
4 _____

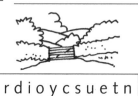
t e l c s a
5 _____

r d i o y c s u e t n
6 _____

r c e t n c o
7 _____

r a a i f s   r p k a
8 _____

2 Look and write.

1
Let's go to the water park!
Yes, great idea!

2
Let's _____!
No, I don't want to.

3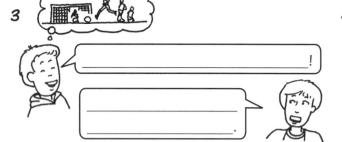
_____!
_____.

4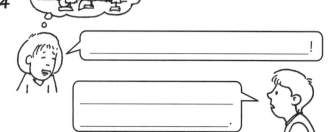
_____!
_____.

3 Write sentences.

I want to …

I want to go to the circus.

_____.

_____.

_____.

I don't want to …

I don't want to go to the beach.

_____.

_____.

_____.

Lesson 1 Vocabulary presentation

Lesson 2

4 Read and write the correct sentences.

1 Davina wants to see Freddie tomorrow.
No, <u>Davina wants to see Freddie now.</u>

2 Davina and Freddie meet in the internet café.
No, _____.

3 Davina is very happy.
No, _____.

4 Davina sends the gym instructor a text message.
No, _____.

5 Jack sees the gym instructor's black car.
No, _____.

6 The driver gives Davina a box of chocolates.
No, _____.

5 Read and write the story summary.

| driver   sorry   burger bar   code   angry   car   message   paper   ~~mobile phone~~ |

In the burger bar

Davina calls her (1) <u>mobile phone</u> and Freddie answers. Davina and Freddie meet in the (2) _____. At first Davina is very (3) _____. Then Davina and Freddie both say they're (4) _____. Davina sends a text (5) _____ to Q to sell the magic emerald. Suddenly Q's black (6) _____ appears. The (7) _____ gives Davina a piece of (8) _____ with a message in secret (9) _____.

6 Read and number in order.

Freddie: I'm sorry, too. ☐

Davina: Were you at the gym yesterday afternoon? ☐ 1

Davina: Don't lie! Yes, you were! Was it poison in my water, Freddie? ☐

Freddie: Yes, it was. But at Q's house you were a traitor … ☐

Freddie: No, I wasn't. ☐

Davina: OK. I'm sorry. ☐

Lesson 2 Language input and story

Lesson 3

7 Write about your friends in the chain game.

Yesterday morning Jon was at the internet café.
_____.

Yesterday afternoon _____.
_____.

Yesterday evening _____.
_____.

8 Look, write and say the grammar rap.

Were you ___at the beach___ yesterday morning?
No, I _____. I was _____.

Was he _____ yesterday afternoon?
No, he _____. He _____.

Was she _____ yesterday evening?
No, she _____. She _____. It was _____!

9 Write questions and answers.

1. Were you at the castle yesterday afternoon?
Yes, I was.

2. _____ morning?
No, _____.

3. _____ evening?
Yes, _____.

4. _____ afternoon?
No, _____.

Lesson 3 Communication and grammar

Lesson 4

10 **Listen, match and write.**

Where were Jack and Emily last Saturday?

1 nine o'clock   2 half past eleven   3 one o'clock   4 half past three   5 seven o'clock

a cinema   *b* park   *c* home   *d* pizza restaurant   *e* supermarket

1 At <u>nine o'clock they were at home.</u>   2 At _____.
3 _____.   4 _____.
5 _____.

11 Read and write.

1 Where were you at eight o'clock last Saturday?   <u>I was at home.</u>
2 Where were you at half past ten last Saturday?   _____.
3 Where were you at two o'clock last Saturday?   _____.
4 Where were you at half past five last Saturday?   _____.
5 Where were you at half past seven last Saturday?   _____.

12 **Listen, tick (✔) and say.**

Pronunciation gem

1 I was at the beach at six o'clock. ☐   2 He was in town at four o'clock. ☐

3 She was at school yesterday morning. ☐   4 I was at home at six o'clock. ☐

5 He was at the internet café yesterday evening. ☐   6 She was at the funfair at eight o'clock. ☐

Lesson 4 Communication, grammar and pronunciation

Lesson 5

13 Read and match.

1 They were very thick.   a the towers
2 They were very small.   b the moat
3 They were very high.   c the dungeon
4 It was big and heavy.   d the castle walls
5 It was deep.   e the drawbridge
6 It was very dark.   f the windows
7 It was narrow.   g the wooden gate

14 Look and write.

walls   towers   windows   moat   drawbridge   ~~gate~~   dungeon

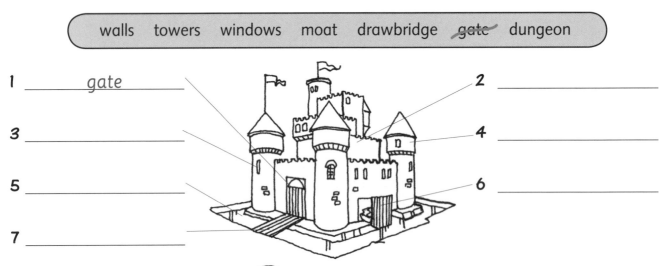

1 _gate_
2 _____
3 _____
4 _____
5 _____
6 _____
7 _____

15 Imagine, draw and write.

The towers were high.
The gate was big.
The moat was deep.

Lesson 6

16 Read and circle.

1 Life in a castle was hard. — (True) / False
2 The castle was warm and dry. — True / False
3 The food was always bad. — True / False
4 It was easy for people to wash. — True / False
5 There were acrobats and musicians. — True / False
6 There were feasts and games. — True / False

17 Read and write Yes, it was. / No, it wasn't.

1 Was the castle cold? _____.
2 Was the castle warm? _____.
3 Was the castle damp? _____.
4 Was the castle light? _____.
5 Was the castle dark? _____.
6 Was the castle smelly? _____.
7 Was the castle quiet? _____.
8 Was the castle noisy? _____.

18 Draw and write.

I think life in a castle was cool!

Lesson 7

19 Read and write the answers. Look at Pupil's Book page 60.

Warwick Castle:	1	Were the towers high?	<u>Yes, they were.</u>
	2	Was the dungeon small?	<u>No, it wasn't.</u>
Cheddar Caves:	3	Were the caves deep?	_____.
	4	Was it very interesting?	_____.
Alton Towers Theme Park:	5	Was the park full of people?	_____.
	6	Was it a rainy day?	_____.
Longleat Safari Park:	7	Were the elephants quiet?	_____.
	8	Were the lions hungry?	_____.

20 Read and write *was* or *were*.

Our school trip last term (1) ___was___ to Warwick Castle. The towers (2) _____ very high and the dungeon (3) _____ enormous. It (4) _____ brilliant! By Daisy.

Our school trip last term (5) _____ to the Cheddar Caves. The caves (6) _____ very deep and dark. They (7) _____ also cold and damp. It (8) _____ very interesting but it (9) _____ also a bit scary! By Oliver.

21 Write about a school trip and draw.

_____
_____
_____
_____

Lesson 7 Intercultural learning

Lesson 8

22 Look and write the dialogue.

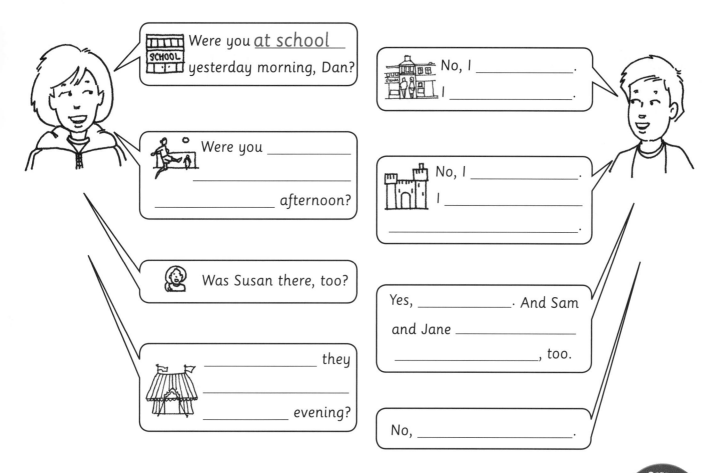

23 Put on the *Grammar Footprints* stickers.

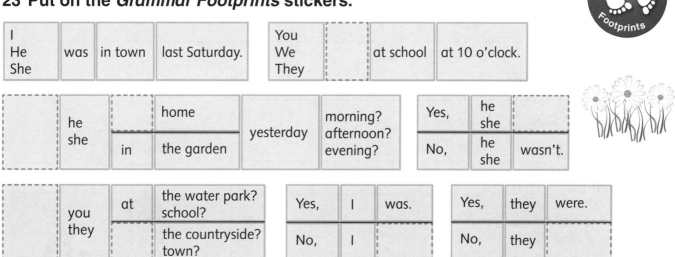

24 Write the answers to the *Footprints quiz.*

1 Name the six places to go.

 safari park   _____   _____

2 Where were you yesterday morning?
_____.

3 Where were you yesterday afternoon?
_____.

4 Where were you yesterday evening?
_____.

5 Write a question about Freddie yesterday afternoon.
_____?

6 Write a question about Jack and Emily last Saturday.
_____?

7 Name three parts of a castle.
_____   _____   _____

8 Write a sentence about life in a castle.
_____.

Assess your work.

My Unit 7 score is: / 10

My work is: _____

I need to: _____

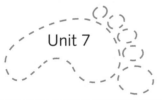
Unit 7

Date: _____

Well done!
Woof!

Lesson 8 Unit review

7 My bilingual dictionary

Main vocabulary

town　　　　　＿＿＿＿＿＿＿＿

countryside　　＿＿＿＿＿＿＿＿

beach　　　　　＿＿＿＿＿＿＿＿

funfair　　　　＿＿＿＿＿＿＿＿

water park　　＿＿＿＿＿＿＿＿

safari park　　＿＿＿＿＿＿＿＿

castle　　　　　＿＿＿＿＿＿＿＿

circus　　　　　＿＿＿＿＿＿＿＿

concert　　　　＿＿＿＿＿＿＿＿

football match　＿＿＿＿＿＿＿＿

burger bar　　＿＿＿＿＿＿＿＿

internet café　＿＿＿＿＿＿＿＿

Other words

yesterday　　　＿＿＿＿＿＿＿＿

last　　　　　　＿＿＿＿＿＿＿＿

argument　　　＿＿＿＿＿＿＿＿

lie　　　　　　　＿＿＿＿＿＿＿＿

sorry　　　　　＿＿＿＿＿＿＿＿

sell　　　　　　＿＿＿＿＿＿＿＿

traitor　　　　　＿＿＿＿＿＿＿＿

code　　　　　＿＿＿＿＿＿＿＿

driver　　　　　＿＿＿＿＿＿＿＿

Extra words I want to remember

In English　　　　**In my language**

＿＿＿＿＿＿＿　　＿＿＿＿＿＿＿

＿＿＿＿＿＿＿　　＿＿＿＿＿＿＿

Footprints fact file: My key words

tower　　　　　＿＿＿＿＿＿＿＿

moat　　　　　＿＿＿＿＿＿＿＿

drawbridge　　＿＿＿＿＿＿＿＿

dungeon　　　＿＿＿＿＿＿＿＿

deep　　　　　＿＿＿＿＿＿＿＿

narrow　　　　＿＿＿＿＿＿＿＿

heavy　　　　　＿＿＿＿＿＿＿＿

damp　　　　　＿＿＿＿＿＿＿＿

8 Things in the past

Lesson 1

1 Find, circle and write.

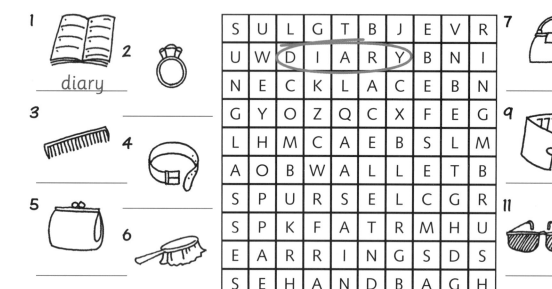

1. diary
2. _____
3. _____
4. _____
5. _____
6. _____
7. _____
8. _____
9. _____
10. _____
11. _____
12. _____

2 Write questions and answers.

1. Whose is the ring?   It's Davina's.
2. _____? _____.
3. _____? _____.
4. _____? _____.

3 Draw and write.

It belongs to me.

The comb belongs to me.
_____.
_____.

It belongs to my friend.

The purse belongs to Lucy.
_____.
_____.

Lesson 1 Vocabulary presentation

Lesson 2

4 Read and number in order.

What did Sam, Jack and Emily tell the detectives?

a A man and a woman were there. They looked suspicious. ☐

b We listened to Davina and Freddie. ☐

c The magic emerald disappeared. ☐

d We visited an exhibition of old pirate treasure. 1

e They decided to sell the magic emerald to Q. ☐

f We followed Davina to the burger bar. ☐

5 Read and write the story summary.

collection   story   funfair   ~~message~~   police station   wallet   gems   police car

At the police station

Jack has Q's (1) __message__ in his (2) _____.
Sam, Jack and Emily decide to go to the (3) _____
and tell their (4) _____. The police say they are
looking for a big (5) _____ of stolen (6) _____.
Sam, Jack and Emily go to the (7) _____ in the
(8) _____ to look for Davina, Freddie and Q.

6 Read, write and say.

talk   ~~follow~~   listened   was

Did you __follow__ Davina to the burger bar?

Yes, we did. And Freddie _____ there.

Did you _____ to Davina and Freddie?

No, we didn't. We _____.

Lesson 2 Language input and story

Lesson 3

7 Look, write and say the grammar rap.

As I ___walked___ to the _____ one day

I _____ my _____ on the way.

Did _____ on the ground?

Yes, _____.

Did _____ in your pocket?

Yes, _____.

I _____ my friends to help, I _____ everywhere.

But, oh dear me, my _____ there.

8 Look and write.

What did they do on the way to school?

They talked.   She skipped.   ~~He listened to music.~~
He picked flowers.   They played with a ball.   She climbed a tree.

1 He listened to music.   2 _____.   3 _____.

4 _____.   5 _____.   6 _____.

9 Draw and write about you.

What did you do on the way to school?

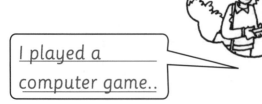

I played a computer game..

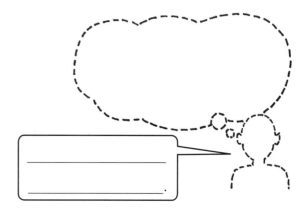

Lesson 3 Communication and grammar

Lesson 4

10 Look, read and write.

What did Jack do on the way to school?

1 He __talked__ to a friend.   2 He _____ his wallet.

What did Emily do on the way to school?

3 She _____ with a ball.   4 She _____ to music.

11 Read and write *Yes, I did* or *No, I didn't*.

1 Did you talk to a friend on the way to school?   2 Did you listen to music?
   _____.   _____.

3 Did you play a computer game?   4 Did you drop your school bag?
   _____.   _____.

5 Did you pick flowers?   6 Did you climb a tree?
   _____.   _____.

12 Look, write and say.

| ~~followed~~ looked skipped climbed helped listened dropped |
| talked phoned played |

/d/
___followed___ _____

_____ _____

_____ _____

/t/
_____ _____

_____ _____

_____ _____

Lesson 4 Communication, grammar and pronunciation

Lesson 5

13 Read and write.

places   clothes   objects   people   food   ~~stories~~

1 We learn about history from ___stories___ of famous people and events.
2 We learn about history from _____, such as castles.
3 We learn about history from the way _____ lived and worked.
4 We learn about history from people's _____, such as their shoes, coats and hats.
5 We learn about history from people's _____ and the way they cooked.
6 We learn about history from the _____ people used in their daily lives.

14 Look and write.

1 a  b
camera

a People _used this camera in the past._
b People _use this camera now._

2 a  b
watch

a People _____.
b People _____.

3 a b
key

a _____.
b _____.

4 a b
diary

a _____.
b _____.

15 Choose, draw and write.

 a b

People used handbag **a** in the past.
People use handbag **b** now.

Lesson 6

16 Read and match.

1 At two months ...   a I walked.
2 At eight months ....   b I hopped.
3 At one year ...   c I kicked a ball.
4 At two years ...   d I smiled.
5 At three years ...   e I talked.
6 At four years ...   f I crawled.

17 Read and write *Yes, I did* or *No, I didn't*.

1 Did you smile at two months?   _____.
2 Did you crawl at eight months?   _____.
3 Did you walk at eight months?   _____.
4 Did you talk at two years?   _____.
5 Did you hop at three years?   _____.
6 Did you climb at four years?   _____.

18 Write and draw.

At five years, I started to read.
At six years, I started to play computer games.

Lesson 7

19 Read and write the answers. Look at Pupil's Book page 68.

1 Did Daisy play a lot?   Yes, she did.
2 Did Leo walk at ten months?   No, he didn't.
3 Did Oliver talk a lot?   _____.
4 Did Amy crawl at six months?   _____.
5 Did Daisy talk at nine months?   _____.
6 Did Leo like nursery school?   _____.
7 Did Amy smile a lot?   _____.
8 Did Oliver like biscuits?   _____.

20 Look and write.

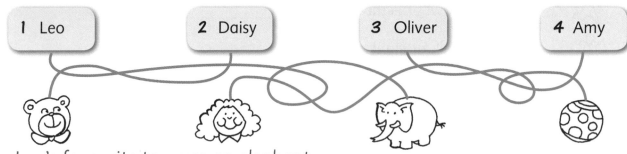

1 Leo's favourite toy was an elephant.
2 _____.
3 _____.
4 _____.

21 Write and draw.

My dad says I was a happy baby. I crawled at nine months and I walked at a year. I liked chocolate and my favourite toy was a car. When I was three, I started to go to nursery school.

Lesson 8

22 Look and write the dialogue.

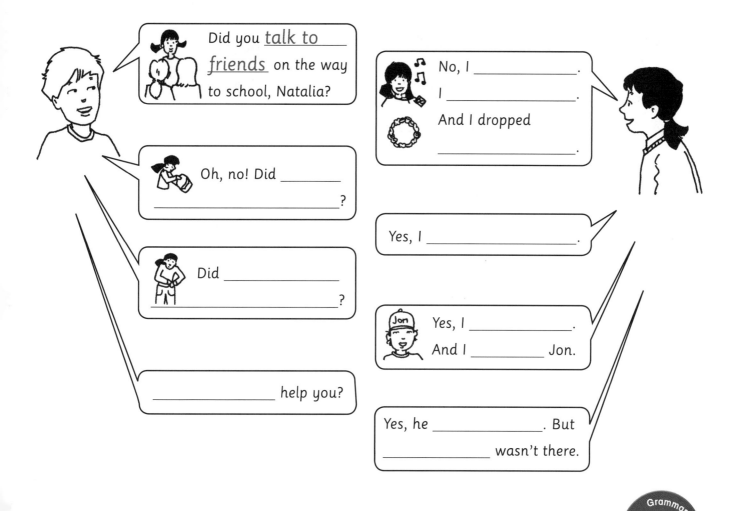

23 Put on the Grammar Footprints stickers.

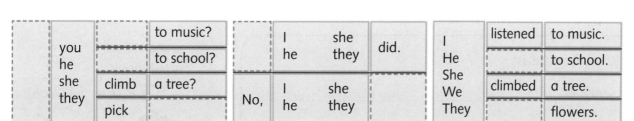

Lesson 8 Unit review

24 Write the answers to the *Footprints quiz.*

1 Name the six things people use or wear every day.

 sunglasses   _____   _____

_____   _____   _____

2 Write what you did on the way to school.

_____.

3 Did Jack drop his sunglasses on the way to school?

_____.

4 Did Emily listen to music on the way to school?

_____.

5 Write three things we learn about history from.

_____.

6 Write a sentence about the camera.

_____.

7 Write a sentence about the watch.

_____.

8 Write two sentences about when you were a baby.

_____.

_____.

Assess your work.

My Unit 8 score is: _____ / 10

My work is: _____

I need to: _____

Date: _____

 Unit 8

Well done!

Woof!

Lesson 8 Unit review

8 My bilingual dictionary

Main vocabulary

handbag _____

diary _____

wallet _____

purse _____

brush _____

comb _____

belt _____

sunglasses _____

ring _____

earrings _____

necklace _____

bracelet _____

Footprints fact file: My key words

history _____

past _____

events _____

people _____

places _____

clothes _____

objects _____

detective _____

Other words

police station _____

suspicious _____

stolen _____

disappear _____

ground _____

pocket _____

Extra words I want to remember

In English	In my language
_____	_____
_____	_____
_____	_____
_____	_____
_____	_____
_____	_____
_____	_____
_____	_____
_____	_____
_____	_____
_____	_____
_____	_____
_____	_____
_____	_____

9 Things I like doing

Lesson 1

1 Look and write.

> dive   camp   cook   dress up   make models   collect shells   travel   do jigsaw puzzles

1 _dress up_
2 _____
3 _____
4 _____
5 _____
6 _____
7 _____
8 _____

2 Write sentences.

What do they do in the holidays?

1 She _has picnics with friends._
2 He _____.
3 They _____.
4 _____.
5 _____.
6 _____.

3 Write about you.

What do you do in the holidays?

Always	Sometimes	Never
I always read books.	I sometimes travel.	I never dress up.
_____	_____	_____
_____	_____	_____
_____	_____	_____

Lesson 1 Vocabulary presentation

Lesson 2

4 Read and write the correct sentences.

1. Sam, Jack, Emily and Rusty go to the safari park.
   No, _they go to the funfair._

2. Jack and Emily talk to Davina.
   No, _____.

3. Rusty runs away from the detectives.
   No, _____.

4. Rusty barks at Freddie.
   No, _____.

5. Rusty wants some water.
   No, _____.

6. Sam, Jack and Emily are under arrest.
   No, _____.

5 Read and write the story summary.

magic emerald   funfair   everywhere   biscuit   detectives   ~~car~~

A biscuit for Rusty

The detectives stop the (1) ___car___ and walk to the (2) _____ with Sam, Jack, Emily and Rusty. They look (3) _____ for Davina, Freddie and Q. Jack and Emily talk to the (4) _____. Suddenly Rusty runs away from Sam. He sits down in front of Davina and barks. Rusty wants a biscuit. Q asks Freddie for the (5) _____ but it is too late. Davina, Freddie and Q are under arrest. Rusty really deserves a (6) _____ now!

6 Read, write and say.

bike   detectives   ~~jigsaw puzzles~~

What do you like doing?

I like doing _jigsaw puzzles_.

I think you like being _____, too!

And I like riding my _____.

Lesson 2 Language input and story

Lesson 3

7 Look, write and say the grammar rap.

I like __playing board games__. I like _____, too.
But I don't like _____. What about you?
Do you like _____?
   Yes, _____.
Do _____?
   No, _____.
Do _____?
   Yes, _____.
I like _____. I _____, too.
But _____. They're hard to do!

8 Write and answer *Yes, I do* or *No, I don't*.

1. __Do you like camping?__ _____
2. _____? _____
3. _____? _____
4. _____? _____
5. _____? _____
6. _____? _____

9 Write about you.

I like ...

__I like riding my bike.__
_____.
_____.
_____.

I don't like ...

__I don't like playing football.__
_____.
_____.
_____.

Lesson 3 Communication and grammar

Lesson 4

10 Look and write.

1 Jack <u>likes camping.</u>   2 He <u>doesn't like having picnics.</u>

3 He _____.   4 He _____.

5 Emily _____.   6 She _____.

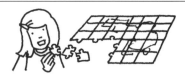 

7 _____.   8 _____.

11 Read, write and say.

 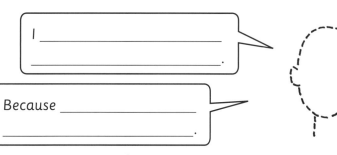

12 Say and draw ↗ up or down ↘ .

Pronunciation gem

1 Do you like reading? ↗   2 What do you like doing? ↘

3 Do you like camping?   4 What about you?

5 Do you like cooking?   6 Why?

7 What do you like doing?   8 Do you like collecting shells?

Lesson 4 Communication, grammar and pronunciation

Lesson 5

13 Read and match.

1 Coasts are where …
2 Coasts change …
3 At high tide …
4 At low tide …
5 Sometimes the waves …
6 But at other times the sea …
7 Rocky beaches have …
8 Sandy beaches have …

a the sea comes in.
b is calm.
c rocks and rock pools
d the land and the sea meet.
e sand.
f the sea goes out.
g all the time.
h are big.

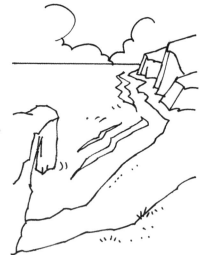

14 Look and write.

shell   seaweed   starfish   crab   mussel   turtle

1 _____mussel_____

2 _____

3 _____

4 _____

5 _____

6 _____

15 Write and draw.

Lesson 5 Content and personalisation

Lesson 6

16 Read and tick (✔) or cross (✘).

✔ = Do this when you go to the beach.
✘ = Don't do this when you go to the beach.

1 Swim when the flag is green.   ✔
2 Throw sand.   ✘
3 Take your pet.   ☐
4 Swim when the flag is red.   ☐
5 Put on sun cream.   ☐
6 Wear a sun hat.   ☐
7 Drink water.   ☐
8 Leave rubbish on the beach.   ☐

17 Read and write *Yes, I do* or *No, I don't*.

When you go to the beach …

1 Do you sit in the shade some of the time?   _____.
2 Do you stay in the sun at midday?   _____.
3 Do you drink water?   _____.
4 Do you watch the tide?   _____.
5 Do you play ball games near other people?   _____.
6 Do you swim when the flag is red?   _____.

18 Write and draw.

When I go to the beach, I put on sun cream. ✔
I wear a sun hat. ✔
I don't throw sand. ✘
I don't swim when the flag is red. ✘

Lesson 6 Content and personalisation

Lesson 7

19 Read and write the answers. Look at Pupil's Book page 76.

1 Does Daisy like reading? Yes, she does.
2 Does Leo like helping at home? No, he doesn't.
3 Does Amy like watching TV? _____.
4 Does Oliver like having picnics? _____.
5 Does Amy like listening to music? _____.
6 Does Oliver like collecting shells? _____.
7 Does Leo like doing jigsaws? _____.
8 Does Daisy like shopping? _____.

20 Look and write.

	Daisy	Leo	Amy	Oliver
Likes ... ☺	reading	playing computer games	playing board games	swimming
Doesn't like ... ☹	shopping	helping at home	listening to music	going sightseeing

1 Daisy <u>likes reading but she doesn't like shopping.</u>
2 Leo _____.
3 Amy _____.
4 Oliver _____.

21 Write and draw.

In the holidays I like going to the cinema and riding my bike in the park. It's fun. I also like reading and watching TV. I don't like listening to music. It's boring.

Lesson 8

22 Look and write the dialogue.

23 Put on the *Grammar Footprints* stickers.

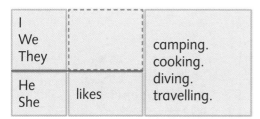

Lesson 8 Unit review

24 Write the answers to the *Footprints quiz*.

1 Name the six holiday activities.

 camp _____ _____

 _____ _____ _____

2 Do you like reading in the holidays?
_____.

3 Do you like helping at home in the holidays?
_____.

4 Write two sentences about what you like doing in the holidays.
_____.
_____.

5 Write two sentences about what you don't like doing in the holidays.
_____.
_____.

6 Write three things you can find on beaches.

 _____ _____ _____

7 Write two rules for the beach.
_____.

8 Write a sentence about what you like doing when you go to the beach.
_____.

Assess your work.

My Unit 9 score is: _____ / 10

My work is: _____

I need to: _____

Unit 9

Date: _____

Well done!

Woof!

9 My bilingual dictionary

Main vocabulary

travel _____

go sightseeing _____

camp _____

cook _____

have picnics _____

take photos _____

collect shells _____

dive _____

play board games _____

do jigsaw puzzles _____

make models _____

dress up _____

Footprints fact file: My key words

high tide _____

low tide _____

wave _____

rocky _____

sandy _____

crab _____

seaweed _____

starfish _____

Other words

abroad _____

under arrest _____

deserve _____

boring _____

Extra words I want to remember

In English	In my language

93

Lesson 6   Make and play with *My Little Fact File of Sleep*.

4

When I have enough sleep, I feel in a _____ mood.

When I don't have enough sleep, I feel in a _____ mood.

5

Before I go to sleep, I always _____.

8

And when I wake up after _____ hours of sleep, I'm ready for another day!

My Little Fact File of **Sleep**

By _____

Zzzzzz!

3

I go to bed at _____.

I wake up at _____.

I sleep for _____ hours.

6

Before I go to sleep, I sometimes _____.

2

I am a _____. I need _____ hours of sleep a day.

7

Before I go to sleep, I never _____.

Lesson 6   Make and play with *My Little Fact File of Food*.

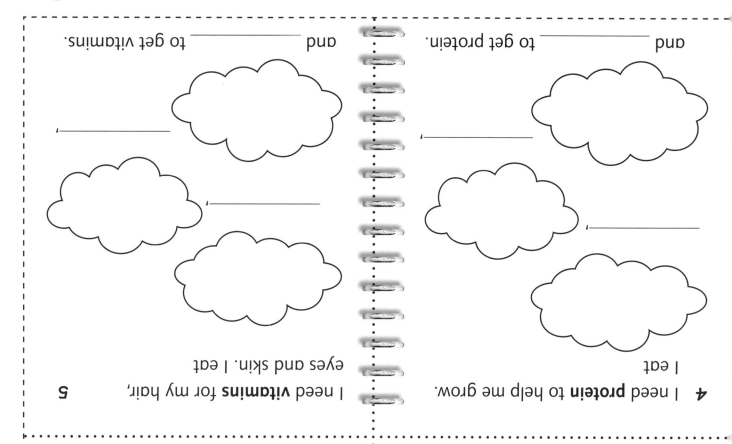

4 I need **protein** to help me grow.
I eat _____ and _____ to get protein.

5 I need **vitamins** for my hair,
eyes and skin. I eat _____ and _____ to get vitamins.

8

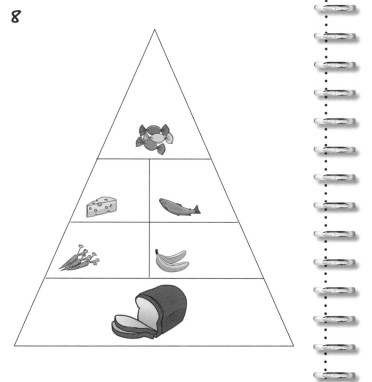

My Little Fact File of Food

By _____

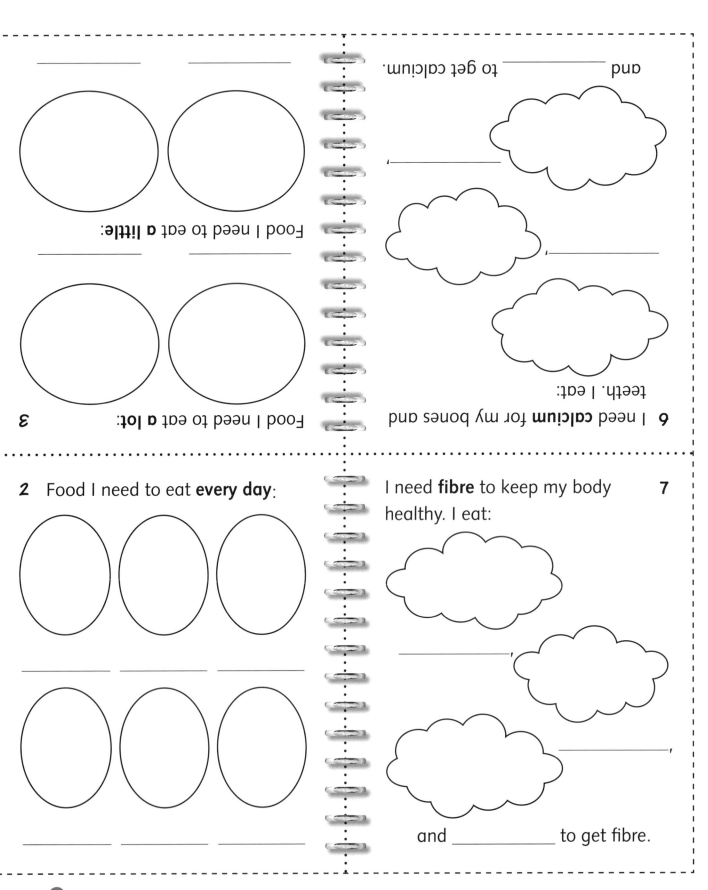

Lesson 6 — Make and play with *My Little Fact File of Transport*.

(upside-down, top half of page)

I _____ and I _____ .

When I go by _____ ,

I go to _____ by _____ .

5 I go to _____ by _____ .

4

(right-side up, bottom half)

8

When I go by _____ ,
I _____ .

My favourite form of transport is a
_____ .

My Little Fact File of Transport

By _____

6

When I go by _____,

I _____

and I _____.

3

I go to _____
by _____.

I go to _____
by _____.

---

2 Transport I use.

○ ○ ○
___ ___ ___

○ ○ ○
___ ___ ___

7

I go to _____
by _____.

I go to _____
by _____.

100

4 Lesson 6 Make and play with *My Little Fact File of Computers*.

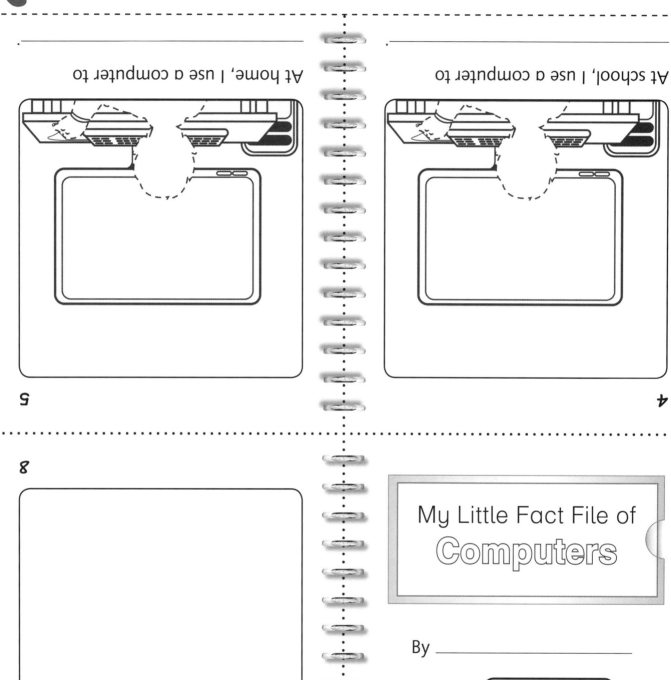

At school, I use a computer to

4

At home, I use a computer to

5

8

I use a computer to write

My Little Fact File of
Computers

By _____

It's got a monitor, a screen, a keyboard, a mouse and a printer.

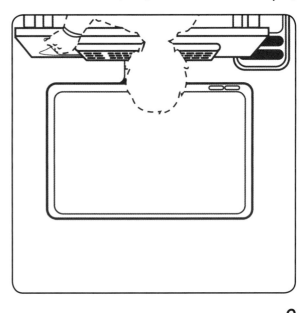

3 _____

2 _____

I also use a computer to _____.

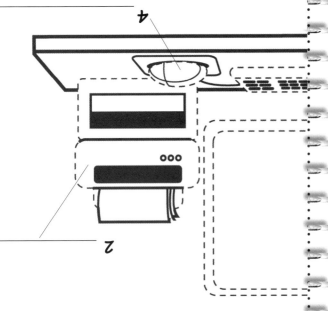

6

1 _____
2
3 _____

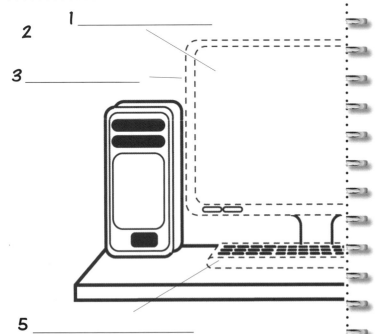

5 _____

At school, the computer I use is like this.

When I create a document, 7
I use different _____.

I use different **E p w** _____.

SJk

I use different ᴇEEE _____.

I also use **sjk** _____

and *sjk* _____.

Lesson 6   Make and play with *My Little Fact File of Muscles*.

4

Some muscles, like the ones in my _____ and _____ are called voluntary muscles.

5

Some muscles, like the ones in my _____ and _____ are called involuntary muscles.

8 My muscles work like this.

1 _____
2 _____
3 _____
4 _____

My Little Fact File of
Muscles

By _____

2

My body has more than ____ muscles.

3 I have muscles in my:

_____ _____

_____ _____

_____ _____

6 I use my muscles to _____

and to _____.

7 I also use my muscles to

and to _____.

Lesson 6   Make and play with *My Little Fact File of the Five Senses*.

[Page 5 — upside down]

_____.

I _____ with my _____.
I use my _____ to _____.

[Page 4 — upside down]

_____.

I _____ with my _____.
I use my _____ to _____.

8

I like _____ things such as _____.

I don't like _____ things such as _____.

My Little Fact File of the Five Senses

By _____

105

3

I _____ with my _____. I use my _____ to _____.

6

I _____ with my _____. I use my _____ to _____.

2 I have five senses. They are

_____, _____, _____, _____,

and _____.

I _____ with my _____. **7**

1 _____   2 _____

3 _____

4 _____

5 _____

Lesson 6 — Make and play with *My Little Fact File of Castles*.

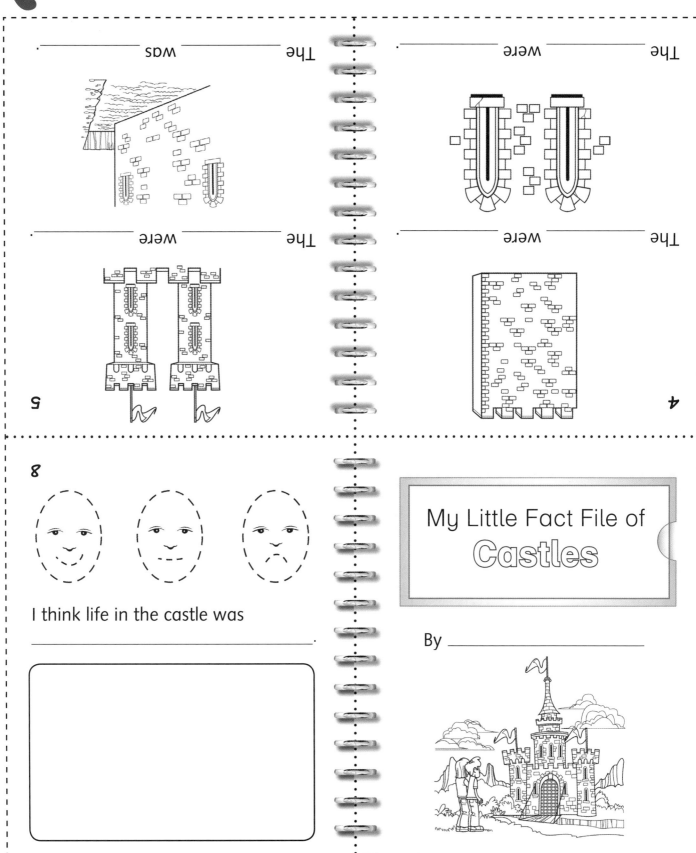

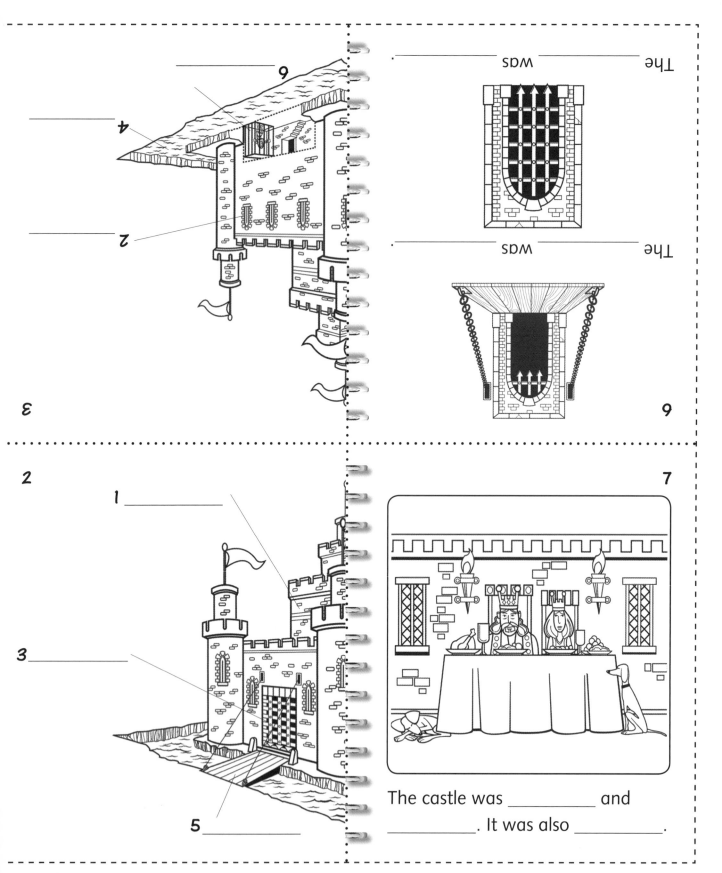

The The was _____.

The was _____.

The castle was _____ and _____. It was also _____.

Lesson 6 — Make and play with *My Little Fact File of Personal History.*

At _____ years, I _____
.

5

At one year, I _____
.

4

8

At _____ years, I _____
.

My Little Fact File of Personal History

By _____

3

At _____ months, I _____
_____.

6

At _____ years, I _____
_____.

2

At _____ months, I _____
_____.

7

At _____ years, I _____
_____.

 **Lesson 6** Make and play with *My Little Fact File of Beaches*.

[Page 5 — upside down] I like _____ on the beach.

[Page 4 — upside down] You can also find _____, _____ and _____.

[Page 8]

My favourite beach is like this.

My Little Fact File of
Beaches

By _____

2

Some beaches are _____.

Some beaches are _____.

3

You can find _____ , _____ and _____ on beaches.

7 When I go to the beach,

I _____.

I don't _____.

6 I also like _____ on the beach.